Driving Strom Thurmond

by Buddy Wilkes

ISBN-13: 978-1511712866
ISBN-10: 151172864
Copyright 2015

Part I

1. Old Tan Briefcase
2. Chitlin' Strut
3. The Autograph
4. The Peach Festival
5. Nursing Home
6. Clear on the Right
7. Ain't No Mortgage
8. Saved by the Blonde
9. Boys State
10. Soup
11. We Have Always Denied That

Part II

Part I

By the time World War II broke out, Strom Thurmond had already been a teacher, coach, county superintendent of education, lawyer, city attorney, county attorney, state senator, and circuit judge. Then he joined the D-Day Invasion of Normandy, earning a chestful of medals.

After the war he came back home to Edgefield County, South Carolina and jumped right back into politics feet first, winning the election for Governor in 1946. He ran for president in 1948; in 1954 he became a US Senator for life, serving until 2003, the year he died at the age of 100.

During his many years as Senator, Agents of the South Carolina Law Enforcement Division (SLED) drove Strom Thurmond anywhere he wanted to go. In the late 1990's, I had my turn at driving the

Senator, when he was famous for three things: constituent service, being as old as Methuselah, and for being somewhat fond of the ladies.

1.   Old Tan Briefcase

The briefing was simple: don't forget the hat, don't be late, and hide your blue light.

The old highway patrol hat was, I suppose, actually in style at some point in history. It was sort of a small cowboy hat with a brim that flipped upwards all the way around, just like the one worn by Sheriff Buford T. Justice in Smokey and the Bandit. The hat stayed in the Officer of the Day Quarters in the basement of SLED when the Senator was in Washington. When an Agent picked him up, the hat was always in the back seat, just in case he asked for it.

Strom Thurmond was always in a hurry, and I don't think we fooled him with our excuses about the blue lights. He told me once with a touch of sarcasm that he was going to appropriate some money so the Chief could buy some more blue lights, since all ours seemed to be broken.

Fully briefed, hat on the back seat, blue light in trunk, I arrived at the Columbia Airport to pick him up for the first time.

The plane taxied up to the terminal and folks started coming down the ramp and into the terminal. I had the passageway staked out. The Senator got halfway down the narrow corridor and stopped, thus halting the exit of every passenger behind him.

He set his old tan leather briefcase on the floor. It looked like something Indiana

Jones would carry, other than the crinkled and faded red white and blue Strom Thurmond campaign sticker.

He fumbled and dug through the case, oblivious to the rest of the passengers patiently queued up behind him, smiling. No one offered to tell, or even ask, Senator Strom Thurmond to move out of the way. Much later, after many miles and days spent escorting the Senator around the state, I understood why. Most probably, every person waiting in that line behind him knew someone that Senator Thurmond had helped in some way. If you had a problem with the government – veterans' benefits, social security, you name it - his office helped you. No matter who you were, you got help when you called the Senator's office. It would have been the height of impropriety to show anything but due deference to the Senator.

I introduced myself as Agent Buddy Wilkes and received a surprisingly firm handshake, given the fact that he was two years older than dirt by this time.

"Wilkes. W,I,L,K,E,S," he spelled out loud. He moved over just a bit, so everyone getting off the plane would have to walk right by us. Most folks smiled and nodded a few shouted hellos, a few shook hands with the Senator and kept on going. Then I saw why he was stalling. A gorgeous blonde in a business suit came by in the parade getting off the plane, her eyes straight ahead. The Senator called to her and introduced me as "his SLED Agent," and asked me, so she would be sure to hear, if it would be alright to give his friend a ride.

"Yes sir, no problem," I said.

She thanked us very much, but explained that someone was picking her up.

The Senator chatted her up all the way to the luggage carousel where she parted company to catch her ride, a subtle look of relief on her face.

We grabbed his luggage and jogged out to the car, conveniently parked right outside the door. When you were driving Strom Thurmond, you parked where you wanted.

2.   Chitlin' Strut

As we pulled out of his driveway early one morning and headed towards Salley, South Carolina, home of the Chitlin' Strut, Senator Thurmond told me "sometimes you have to go amongst the unwashed masses."

The proper name for pig intestines is "chitterlings." The recipe is simple: boil the feces out of them, then deep fry in boiling hot hog fat.

With the windows up and the air conditioner on, I could smell the Chitlin' Strut from the outer suburbs of Salley. Tears came to my eyes.

As usual, people flocked to the car as soon as we stopped. Some came right up to him. Others stayed back and made eye contact with me, seeking my permission, by slight expression or gesture, to approach the Senator. My signal always indicated "yes." It was always surprising to me that he knew so many people by name.

Handshakes, how's so-and-so doing, pictures, autographs. People with money acted like they were old friends with the Senator, and they probably were. Working people came in droves to thank him for straightening out mama's disability check or daddy's veterans' benefits. Some people were too shy to approach, but looked on from a distance and whispered among themselves.

It was like being with Elvis.

Somebody handed the Senator a bag of fresh-fried pig skins, and he handed them to me. Grease had soaked through the brown paper bag and slowly dripped from the bottom. They were delicious.

A cub reporter covering the Chitlin' Strut saw her opportunity to interview the longest-serving Senator in the history of the United States.

I knew she was a cub reporter because she didn't rate a cameraman. She lugged her own video camera and tripod about, a rig that weighed as much as she did.

The Senator agreed to the interview without hesitation, and the young lady set her tripod up right where they stood, directly in front of the exhaust fan of the world's largest chitlin' kitchen. The huge fan turned slowly, wop, wop, wop, and pushed the heat and smell of frying chitlins our way.

The Senator did not seem to notice. He stood up straight as a post for the camera. I eased off to the side so I could breathe.

After the short interview, we headed towards the old Salley schoolhouse across the way. Crowds of people milled about the hardwood and plaster hallways and classrooms, filled with tables piled with arts and crafts and yard sale stuff.

While browsing, I looked at a pair of plastic pearl earrings, the old-timey type that clamped to your ears. A few minutes later, I noticed the Senator at the same table. He paid the lady the 5 cent price, and removed the masking tape price tag. As we were leaving the building, he took the earrings out of his coat pocket and presented them to me.

"Take these ear bobs to yo' wife," he said.

"Well thank you, Senator. She'll like those," I answered.

"We better hurry up - we gone be late," he said with a purpose, and away we went to the next event.

3.   The Autograph

Now the Senator never minded giving anyone an autograph. He'd say "glad to do it. Now who do I make this out to?"

But I guess he didn't like being told what to do.

Another Agent, a high-ranking one, brought me a picture one day. He wanted me to get the Senator to sign it. No problem.

The next day, after the Senator and I got on the road, I handed him the big envelope and told him the deal.

He opened it up and took a look. Inside was an 8 by 10 color glossy print of the Senator standing with a group of people. The photo was inside a cardboard template cut out where the Agent wanted him to sign, on a certain area of the photo below the people.

The Agent had written detailed instructions above the cut-out, down to the exact words the Senator was supposed to write. Quite a large bunch of words.

The Senator studied the instructions and flipped to the picture. Back to the instructions, back to the picture. Back to the instructions, back to the picture.

His look of aggravation disappeared as he removed the picture and tossed the template towards the back seat.

He took out his pen and wrote and wrote, completely covering the smiling faces with his old-school cursive.

"There," he pronounced, obviously pleased with himself. He slid the photo back into the envelope, tossed it in the back seat, and went to reading his newspaper.

"We better hurry up. We gone be late."

"Yes sir," I answered automatically, as I stepped on the gas.

4. The Peach Festival

We got to Johnston just in time for the start of the parade. The welcome sign proclaimed the tiny little town to be the "Peach Capital of the World."

Bands were warming up and farm tractors were pulling decorated wagons full of people up and down the side roads. The parade was just about staged up, ready for the trip down Main Street.

A proper-looking fellow trotted up to the car and introduced himself.

"Your horse is ready, Senator," he said, a man on a mission.

I grabbed the Senator's hat off the back seat and handed it to him. The proper fellow boosted him up onto the horse, a tall brown model with a western saddle strapped on his back. The Senator towered over everyone.

"You follow right in behind me!" he shouted. I gestured a "thumbs up" and jumped behind the wheel. We were off.

The chaos turned to order. The bands and tractors and wagons were all headed in the same direction now, towards the town square.

As we all moved along, the proper fellow ran up to my car.

"Can I ride with you? That's my horse Senator Thurmond is riding." He sounded worried.

"Sure. Hop in," I answered.

He introduced himself again, and seemed a little disappointed when I told him that I was not a Secret Service Agent. But he was preoccupied. He never took his eyes off the Senator and that horse.

It seemed the Senator had decided on the spur of the moment that he was going to ride the horse in the parade. And, since we had arrived so late, there had been no time for instructions on how to handle this particular horse. And, since no one ever told Strom Thurmond "no," there he went, waving to the crowd, riding high in the saddle.

The proper fellow was scared to death that the Senator was going to fall off. Being over 90 years old, that would not have been a good thing. My passenger was so nervous his back never touched the seat; he held the dashboard in a death grip.

A platoon of Civil War re-enactors marched in front of the Senator. Without notice, they stopped in place and fired off a salute, en masse, from their big bore rifles. It sounded like a hundred pounds of dynamite going off.

The horse started, then sort of squatted down a little and began backing up.

"Oh Lord. Oh Lord." The poor fellow was about to have a stroke.

He opened his door and was just about to step out when the soldiers started back to marching and the horse took off behind them.

His face was tortured as he shut his door and sat there, leaning forward and wringing his hands. He explained that this horse was trained to back up when you tightened up on the reins, something of which the Senator was not aware.

"Blam! Blam! Blam!" Another volley. As the Senator pulled back on the reins and the horse backed up, the saddle slipped about 15 degrees to the right.

"Oh Lord. Oh Lord," the poor man whined.

The Senator never missed a lick, still sitting straight up in the tilted saddle. My passenger started to open his door twice more, but each time the parade took off again.

I reassured him that the Senator was an expert horseman, and not to worry. He finally leaned back and relaxed a little. I really had no idea what kind of rider the Senator was. But this guy needed some relief and I gave it to him.

"Look. He's not worried - he hasn't missed a wave," I said in my most confident tone.

The saddle seemed to stay in its position, 15 degrees off top dead center. The soldiers fired a couple of more volleys and the crowd got larger and closer as we passed through the middle of town. The horse back-stepped and side-stepped and jittered about.

When we got to the end, the parade turned down a side street toward the railroad tracks. The poor fellow jumped out of the car and trotted towards the Senator, who had stopped the horse right beside a big ditch that ran parallel to the railroad track. This greatly complicated the poor fellow's task of helping the Senator down off the horse. Once his feet were on the ground, the Senator shook the guy's hand and took off to work the crowd.

The poor fellow, and the horse, looked like they needed a drink.

5.   Nursing Home

In 1995, I believe it was, I took the Senator to the Batesburg Christmas Parade. He rode with some folks in a convertible, and I followed behind in my SLED car.

At the end of the line, he hopped back in the car with me. As we turned around in a parking lot, he spotted a row of old folks in wheelchairs by the curb, bundled up in blankets.

"Let's stop here a minute," the Senator said as he opened the door and hopped out. He started at one end of the row and worked his way to the last one.

"Strom Thurmond, how you doin'? Strom Thurmond, how you doin'?"

A small crowd gathered, and someone pointed out to the Senator that there was another group, too feeble to come outside, watching from inside the lobby of the building at the other end of the parking lot.

"Let's go speak to 'em," he said, and away we went.

A hawkish, no-nonsense looking woman in a business suit greeted the Senator at the door and very efficiently introduced herself. She explained that she was the manager of the brand new extended care facility.

The Senator was clearly not familiar with this terminology and interrupted her two or three sentences into her canned speech.

"Is this a nursing home?"

"No sir. This is an extended care facility," she corrected, perturbed, and continued with her speech, only to be interrupted again after a minute or so.

"Is this a nursing home?"

She gave him the same answer as before. After the third inquiry, she relented.

"Yes sir. This is a nursing home," she answered, with obvious exasperation.

The Senator looked pleased that he had finally established that this was in fact a nursing home. He made his way to the old folks lined up in wheelchairs by the front window, too sick and feeble to go outside to see the parade.

"Strom Thurmond, how you doin'? Strom Thurmond, how you doin'?" he said loudly, as he shook each hand vigorously.

He got to the end of the row to a poor old lady with glazed over eyes, obviously not in full command of her faculties.

"Ma'am, you know who I am?" he asked, as he bent over to face her, shaking her hand.

She stared at him for a few seconds and slightly shook her head.

"No, I don't," she spoke deliberately. "But if you go up to that counter, they can tell you."

"We better hurry up. We gon' be late."

6. Clear on the Right

Strom Thurmond was sometimes late, but he was always in a hurry.

One Sunday afternoon we got to the Columbia Airport early. We got all the way to the gate and the plane wasn't even there yet. The Senator started looking at his watch and his feet started shuffling about.

"I think we got time to go see Strom Jr. down at the University," he said, almost to himself, as he took off walking towards the exit and the car.

We hopped in the car and took off. Before we had gone ten feet he was telling me to hurry up. I did so. I knew that if you could ever get away with driving like Richard Petty, it was when you had Strom Thurmond with you. I actually wished I'd been stopped sometimes, just for the entertainment value of seeing the look on the officer's face when he saw my passenger.

"See those people up ahead of us? They ain't in a hurry like we are. Go on 'round 'em!"

We were making tracks. The Senator said enthusiastically "you be the pilot and I'll be the navigator!"

We came up to an intersection and the light turned orange when we were a hundred yards away.

"You can make that - go 'head!"

I blew through a few red lights, slowing down long enough to make sure I wasn't going to plow into some hapless citizen who wasn't in a hurry like we were. Slowing down like that did not suit the Senator.

"Clear on the right!" he hollered, as we approached the next intersection. We got into a pattern. I'd look left and he'd look right. After about the third "clear on the right!" I happened to look in that direction, only to see the Senator reading his newspaper.

I broke out in a cold sweat. If we wrecked and the Senator got hurt, I was dead meat. All the winks and nods about driving the Senator the speed limit would be instantly replaced with the rules and regulations concerning wanton disregard for safety.

I kept going, and I kept going fast. But I paid no more attention to the "clear on the rights." As we approached one intersection, the Senator said "stop at the next one, I need to get in the back seat."

One car was already stopped. We screeched to a halt right beside it, front brakes smoking. The Senator hopped out, opened the back door, and dived in.

"Go 'head!" he shouted.

The light turned green at that instant and we took off. The car beside us just sat there, the driver most probably in a state of confusion over what he had just seen.

He wanted in the back seat so he could re-gift a few Christmas presents he'd accumulated on this trip home to South Carolina. By the time we went through Five Points he was done updating the "to" and "from" cards. A few more blocks and we rolled into Strom Jr.'s driveway. We stayed all of five minutes, then off again, back towards the airport. We went back through West Columbia at Warp Factor Nine, and never saw a cop. After a virtual jog through the airport, we got to the gate just as the last passengers were boarding.

I really don't know why we were in a hurry anyway. This plane, the Sunday evening flight to Washington, D.C., was not going to leave Strom Thurmond. After he boarded, I sat down to rest for a minute. The old man had worn me out again.

7. Ain't No Mortgage

One day I picked the Senator up at the Columbia Airport. The first words out of his mouth were "we late - we got to hurry." Away we went to Aiken. The Senator had a speaking engagement, there was going to be a press conference, we couldn't be late, hurry up, hurry up.

Between Columbia and Aiken it became apparent that neither one of us knew exactly where we were going. This was before GPS, and cell phones were scarce. I had not been issued one at the time.

"I have always found it best to stop and inquire," advised the Senator.

"Yes sir. We can stop at the Police Department," I answered.

I skidded to a stop out front and ran in the door. I was getting directions to the address when a city policeman burst into the room.

"You with Senator Thurmond?"

I nodded, and he yelled "come on!" as he took off out the door. I took off after him.

The officer sprinted across the front lawn to his patrol car and yelled over his shoulder "follow me!"

As soon as I jumped behind the wheel, the officer took off, burning rubber. I did likewise.

We flew through old neighborhoods, then through a blur of strip malls and restaurants, stopping and starting as needed to avoid collisions. I followed the officer right up to a stage built in front of what looked like condos with white columns and porches. The Senator hopped out and started shaking hands.

The death-defying hurry paid off. The Senator got there just in time to take part in the grand-opening of the new retirement home. State Senator Greg Ryberg introduced Senator Thurmond. At the time, Ryberg wore a huge mustache of the style seen in old photographs, not on real live people. Thurmond came to the podium and gave his usual speech about everything being the finest: South Carolina, Aiken, the new buildings, and Senator Ryberg's mustache.

Following a short press conference, the owner of the retirement home took the

Senator and a small group on a tour. As we boarded the elevator, Thurmond asked the owner "what's the mortgage on this place?"

The owner, conscious of the fact that we were all packed on an elevator, tried to whisper his answer to the Senator but it backfired. He had to say it three times, each time a little louder.

"Ain't no mortgage?!" the Senator asked, incredulous. "Well ain't that something! Ain't got no mortgage!"

"No sir. I paid for it as I had it built," he answered, clearly against his wishes.

For the rest of the tour, which included a reception in the board room, Senator Thurmond could be heard by all present each time he met a new face, passing along the news that "there ain't no mortgage on this place - ain't that something!"

The owner cringed, helpless, each and every time he heard his business being broadcast by the most senior Senator in the United States of America.

8. Saved by the Blonde

Strom and Nancy Thurmond built a very nice, very large brick home in Aiken, not far from her parents' house. Then they separated. They never divorced, but they did not live together for the last many years of his life.

The Senator told me they sold the big new house to a doctor. The Senator retained access to the apartment built above the three car garage on the back of the house. Nancy and the children moved into a brick ranch house down the street.

When the Senior Senator from South Carolina, the President Pro Tem of the United States Senate, came home, this was it - a garage apartment, attached to someone else's house.

One weekend the Senator was home from Washington. As usual, his itinerary was jam-packed. I picked him up late Friday evening from the Columbia Airport and took him to his apartment. Once I got him settled, I found my way down the dim steps to the garage.

The only walk-through door led back into the main house. I figured the doctor and his family wouldn't want me wandering through there. No problem, I'd just go out one of the three garage doors.

I found the control button on the wall and gave it a tap. The garage door opened up and I walked out just as it reached the top. Well, that's not going to work, I thought. I can't leave the garage door wide open. Somebody might steal the Senator's 1978 Ford station wagon, a yellow tank with vinyl woodgrain sides.

I went back to the control button and hit it again. The door started to close, and I walked towards my car parked outside. Just as I got under the door, it went into reverse and opened again. After a couple of times, I figured out that I was tripping an electronic beam aimed across the door opening about three feet off the door.

I hit the "close" button again, and tried stepping over the beam. No luck. I was ready to go. I'd have to be back here early in the morning, and it was getting late. I hit the button one more time, sprinted across the garage, hurdled over the beam while ducking my head low to miss the descending door, and I made it. The Senator was locked up tight, and I hit the road, proud of my ingenuity and athletic ability.

I got there the next morning about 30 minutes early. I parked in the driveway down below the garage apartment and started reading the newspaper, happy to have a little down-time before the hectic day began. All was well.

A while later my pager, cell phone, car radio, and walkie-talkie all went off at once. It was Headquarters.

"Senator Thurmond just called and said you weren't there, and that y'all were going to be late, and he's mad," the stressed-out voice said.

"Well, tell him to come on out - I'm sitting here in his driveway - been here for 30 minutes," I explained.

"He already hung up."

"Well call him back."

"We don't have his number."

"Well I'll blow the siren."

"No - no - don't do that!"

I hung up and stepped out of the car. The Senator stuck his head out of the dormer window and saw me. He was mad as a wet hen.

He was wearing an old-timey white tank top t-shirt and his hair was sticking out in all directions. He bobbed back inside and slammed the window.

A minute or two later he came out the door and stomped my way.

"You late! Now I'm gon' be late! Where you been?" he demanded.

"I've been sitting right here, Senator. I got here early."

"No you wasn't! I looked out the window and you wasn't there," he scolded.

O. K. Get mad at me for nothing. No problem. But don't sit there and tell me I'm lying.   I was a little hot-headed in my younger days, and I'm sure it showed in my face.

I looked him dead in the eye and said "Senator, I'll tell you how long I've been sitting here. I was sitting right here when that blonde-headed woman came out of that door right there and drove off in a white Mustang convertible."

Our eyes were locked. Silence. The Senator looked down at his wristwatch and his anger disappeared. He studied his watch, thinking things through.

In a very pleasant tone, he said "we got some time. Let's go upstairs a minute."

The apartment was one big open room, with a little bathroom by the stairs. A double bed sat all the way at the far end. There was a weight bench and a couple of odd pieces of furniture: a little table for the telephone, and a straight chair from a dining room set. It was so sparse that it echoed.

The Senator started going through his closets and pulling out old hats and t-shirts people had given him over the years.

"Here, take these to yo' chillun."

By the time he was finished I had a double arm full of stuff to take home.

"I reckon we can go now. We got plenty of time."

I don't know who that blonde-headed woman was, but she saved me that day.

9.   Boys State

Palmetto Boys State and Girls State are leadership camps sponsored by the American Legion. Each year, selected rising high school seniors are immersed in mock campaigns and elections for a week. They also get to meet a lot of elected officials. Back in the day, that included Senator Strom Thurmond, who served as the keynote speaker at the banquet held at the end of each camp.

At Girls State, this included hugs and kisses and long-stem roses for teenage girls in evening gowns; at Boys State, firm handshakes and pats on the back.

The Senator used the same speech at both events. At Boys State that year, the kids were unusually enthusiastic.

Senator Thurmond told them they were the finest young men in the state of South Carolina.

The room erupted in cheers and applause.

"And South Carolina is the finest state in the United States!"

The room erupted again, only louder. The Senator was feeding off the crowd.

"And the United States is the finest country in the world!!"

Right on cue, the boys clapped and hollered and cheered. The Senator was really getting into it.

"And this is the finest world in the universe!!!"

The room roared.

"And this is the finest universe in the….in the…y'all some fine boys!!!"

Pandemonium ensued as the Senator took this opportunity to end the speech. Perfect timing; I didn't know what was bigger than a universe either.

10. Soup

One afternoon the Senator finished all of his politicking and had nothing left on his schedule. We went upstairs to his garage apartment towards the end of the day. He was restless. Strom Thurmond required constant motion. He paced and puttered about the room, looked out the window, and paced some more. His face lit up and he sat down by the telephone and brought out his little black book.

"Hello George! Strom Thurmond, how you doin'? Good, good. How's your family? That's good. George, are they having church services tonight? No? Well, alright, good to talk to you."

Undaunted, he went down the list. After the fifth call with the same results, he looked puzzled, and announced "Well. Today's Saturday. No wonder. Let's go get some soup!"

People sitting inside Shoney's spotted the unmarked Crown Vic right away. Then they spotted Strom Thurmond. All eyes were on the Senator as we followed the hostess to our table.

In a commanding voice, the Senator announced to her "I want a big bowl of soup. The biggest bowl you have."

She explained to him that she was the hostess, and that she would send the waitress to take his order. He was having none of it.

"Well can't you bring me a bowl of soup? I want a big bowl of soup," he ordered, demonstrating with his hands how big he wanted the bowl to be.

The hostess felt the heat. Everyone in the room could hear what the Senator said, and all eyes were now on her.

She looked at me, and I said I'd have the same.

She looked back at the Senator, and said "yes sir, it'll be right out."

Everyone in the room chuckled, and the Senator looked around the room, one table at a time, making eye contact and waving.

The soup was there in an instant. The hostess brought two servers with her, and they placed the bowls of soup on the table.

The Senator held his bowl up to eye level, for the benefit of the watching crowd, and loudly announced "why that's the smallest bowl of soup I have ever seen! Have you ever seen such a small bowl of soup? Can't you bring me a big bowl?"

By this time, everyone in the room had stopped eating their own supper, and were enjoying the show. The hostess looked like she wanted to crawl in a hole.

"That's the only size bowl we have, but I can refill it as many times as you'd like," she explained.

"Well, I suppose that'll do, if that's the biggest bowl you have. But that's the smallest bowl of soup I've ever seen!"

As the room broke out in laughter, the poor hostess disappeared into the kitchen.

When that bowl was empty, she asked the Senator if would like some more.

"No thank you ma'am, I'm full. But that was the smallest bowl of soup I ever saw."

Thurmond waved back at the room as we left in a hurry, like we were late to an important meeting. We drove back to his garage apartment, and, now satisfied, he called it a day.

11. We Have Always Denied That

During the 1996 campaign season, I drove the Senator to the fairgrounds in rural Florence County. The event, held in a giant metal barn, was a meeting of Republican go-getters, there to hear a few energizing words from Strom Thurmond. Several TV camera crews and print reporters were on hand, waiting on a tid-bit for their by-line.

As soon as we drove up, people flocked to the car to meet and greet the Senator, Governor David Beasley among them. Most of these folks were old friends, and every one of them owed something to the Senator.

The speeches started with county level folks, then a state senator, then the Governor, who introduced Strom Thurmond. The speeches weren't the main event, however. These folks were here to plot political strategy and raise campaign money, something that happens after the speeches, when the crowd breaks down into smaller groups.

The Senator always had somewhere else to be - and this day was no exception. We made our way back to the car, through the crowds of well-wishers. The Senator stopped to speak to every one of them, but we kept moving.

Just as we got to the car, a reporter introduced herself as being with a big-time newspaper, maybe the New York Times. She had pad and pencil in hand as she asked the Senator some innocuous question about the campaign. Then she led into the real question she had for him.

"Senator, it has long been rumored that you had a child with a black woman years ago, and I would like to get your comment on that."

The Senator did not blink, answering right back, "Ma'am, we have always denied that." Then he looked at me and said "let's go." We hopped in the car and away we went, leaving the reporter, and me, to ponder on that answer. "We have always denied that." So who was this "we," I wondered. To a lawyer, a denial is a technical term. It doesn't mean that something is true or not true. It means that you take the *position* that you deny a thing.

He could have said it was not true, a dirty rumor planted by political enemies. But he didn't. He said "...we have always denied that."

After his death, Strom's daughter by the sixteen-year-old family maid came forward. Essie May Washington-Williams and J. Strom Thurmond had agreed to keep quiet about the matter.

It was revealed that the Senator and Essie Mae stayed in contact throughout the Senator's life. He visited her at South Carolina State College when he was the Governor. She visited him in the Governor's Mansion in Columbia and the U.S. Capitol in Washington. But he never publicly acknowledged her as his daughter.

The media was all a-dither, speculating about lawsuits and DNA tests. Then Strom Jr. spoke. Yes, Essie Mae was their sister, and yes they had all been talking and getting along just fine together. That took the wind out of the "scandal." Her name was added to the Strom Thurmond statue behind the State House, and everyone moved on.

Many people in South Carolina knew about Strom Thurmond's daughter all along. It was something whispered, not spoken. The State Newspaper published a picture of Essie Mae and some of her classmates at SC State. All of the women were obviously mixed-race. Little wonder that Strom's contemporary political enemies never told on him.

Part 2

While writing this book, I thought it would be fitting and proper to give a nod to Strom Thurmond for creating SLED by Executive Order in 1947 while he was the Governor.[1]   I had known about this my whole career, but I had never actually seen the Order.

What I found confused me. According to information published during the administrations of numerous governors and several legislative sessions, SLED was created in 1935, twelve years before Strom Thurmond took office. I kept digging, and found that legendary SLED Chief J. P. Strom, Thurmond's cousin, said the same thing. Even the Strom Thurmond Institute,

---

[1] South Carolina Law Enforcement Division Agency Accountability reports 2001-2009, www.sled.sc.gov.

the keeper of all the Senator's records, reported the same.

In 1975, someone replaced the history of the creation of SLED with the version that is generally accepted today, that Strom Thurmond created it. This sparked an interest in me to take a look into Thurmond's history to see what else I didn't know.

12. Daddy and Uncle Ben

James Strom Thurmond was born December 5, 1902 in Edgefield County, South Carolina. His father, John William Thurmond, was a member of the gentry, and one of the most powerful men in Edgefield County. His loyalty lay with Benjamin Ryan Tillman, one of the most unashamedly racist and brutal men South Carolina has ever known. Since slavery was technically ended, the black majority presented an existential threat that Tillman, the elder Thurmond, and many other like-minded people would not abide. Young Strom Thurmond was exposed to this world view at an early age. "When I grew up, the black people were just all servants,"[2] he explained. Thurmond was proud to recount the fact that as a boy, he learned how to shake hands from Ben Tillman, symbolic of his self-perception as Tillman's ideological successor.

Ben Tillman was part of an organized effort that successfully reasserted white supremacy in South Carolina after Reconstruction through terrorism and murder. Since it operated openly in the light of day, I'm not sure you could call it a conspiracy. In his own words, "it had been the settled purpose of the leading white men

---

[2] The Legend of Strom's Remorse, by Timothy Noah, Slate Magazine, December 16, 2002.

of Edgefield to seize upon the first opportunity that the negroes might offer them to provide a riot and teach the negroes a lesson: as it was generally believed that nothing but bloodshed and a good deal of it could answer the purpose of redeeming the state from negro and carpetbag rule."[3] This movement resulted in the violent deaths of hundreds of black citizens in South Carolina, and caused so many to leave the state their numbers dwindled from a majority to one-third of the population.

Tillman describes one episode in which he and fellow members of the Sweetwater Sabre Club summarily executed Simon Coker, a black state senator, for the crime of urging his brethren to stand up for their rights.

---

[3] The Struggles of 1876, How South Carolina Was Delivered From Carpet-Bag and Negro Rule, page 17, by Senator B. R. Tillman; delivered as a speech on August 25, 1909 at The Redshirt Reunion.

"The negro dropped to his knees and began his petition to that Judge before whom he was so soon to appear, but after a few moments Butler (one of the club members) said, 'You are too long; make ready, men.'"

"All cocked their pistols, and the order 'aim, fire,' was given with the negro still kneeling. It will appear a ruthless and cruel thing to those unacquainted with the environments; but those who are disposed to criticise the actions of the men at Hamburg and Ellenton[4] must first put themselves in the places of the whites who had been trampled in the mire by the carpet-baggers and negroes for eight long years,

---

[4] Author's note: *The Hamburg Massacre and the Ellenton Riot resulted in the deaths of over 100 black citizens at the hands of para-military groups of white citizens bent on re-asserting white supremacy in S. C. politics. Source:* The South Carolina Encyclopedia, edited by Walter Edgar, University of South Carolina Press, 2006, pages 295, 415-416.

and realize that the struggle in which we were engaged meant more than life or death. It involved everything we held dear, Anglo-Saxon civilization included."[5]

Tillman's exploits were well known and obviously admired amongst the voting majority of white people; so much so that he was elected Governor of South Carolina, serving from 1890-1894.

Tillman was the leader of the South Carolina constitutional convention of 1895. He had honed "a gift for arousing white audiences with vindictive and inflammatory speeches," and his goal was "the complete elimination of the Negro from participation in South Carolina politics;" the new Constitution "marked...the end of

---

[5] The Struggles of 1876, page 63.

significant Negro participation in the state's politics for half a century."[6]

The law of the land set forth in the document included that "the marriage of a white person with a negro or mulatto, or person who shall have one-eighth or more negro blood, shall be unlawful and void." That took care of the purity of the Anglo-Saxon race in a legal sense, but somehow did not stop the production of mixed-race babies, as Strom Thurmond would later prove.

Male citizens were allowed to vote, "provided, that [they] can both read and write any Section of this Constitution submitted to [them] by the registration officer or can show that he owns...property in this State assessed at three hundred dollars or more." This section alone

---

[6] *The Question of Race in the South Carolina Constitutional Convention of 1895*, by George B. Tindall, *Journal of Negro History*, Volume 37, Issue 3, July 1952.

prevented virtually any black person from voting. Terrorism and election fraud took care of the rest.

That same year, 1895, Strom Thurmond's father nominated Ben Tillman for the U. S. Senate, where Tillman served from that year until his death in 1918. The Congressional Record of February 26, 1900, includes Senator Tillman in his own words: "We stuffed ballot boxes. We shot them. We are not ashamed of it."

Strom Thurmond described his father's relationship with Ben Tillman in a 1978 interview:

"He was a best friend of Benjamin R. Tillman, he was his attorney, his personal attorney. Tillman relied on him. He was his campaign manager."[7]

---

[7] Interview with Strom Thurmond by James G. Banks, 20 July 1978. A-0334 in the Southern Oral History Program Collection #4007, Southern Historical Collection, Wilson Library, University of North Carolina at Chapel Hill., page 8.

Thurmond told the interviewer that he and his father never had a political disagreement, and described Tillman as "an able man." He was obviously very proud to have been associated with Ben Tillman, and went on to describe how he and his father visited Tillman when Strom was a child:

"...we used to go down to Senator Tillman's, particularly on a Sunday afternoon when he was there. When Congress was not in session. It was just six miles, to go in a buggy down there, you can get there in about an hour. I remember one time we went down there, well he told me, he said--when you get there now, you go up, put your hand out and shake hands with Senator Tillman."

"Well, when I got there...I came up to the man, I'd shake hands with him. Senator Tillman was a stern fellow, very profane too. He looked at me and says, "What do you want?"

"I said, I want to shake hands with you. And he says 'Well, why in the hell don't you shake then.' I shook it several times, I been shaking hands ever since."

Young Thurmond was duly impressed. "He (Tillman) was a very dynamic fellow...the best stump speaker, I guess, the state ever produced."[8]

On March 24, 1897, the elder Thurmond, who was the elected Solicitor at the time, shot and killed his unarmed political enemy, Will Harris. Thurmond was sitting at his desk in his office on the town square in Edgefield; Harris was standing on the threshold of the front door of the building. Harris called Thurmond a "God-damned dog and scoundrel"[9] and Thurmond shot him dead. In an affidavit, Thurmond said that "Mr. Harris' movement of his right hand to hip pocket was distinct

[8] *Id.*, page 13.
[9] The Watchman and Southron, Sumter, SC, March 31, 1987.

and unmistakable, and [I] did not doubt that he would draw and fire instantly."[10] A single shot went through Harris' heart.[11]

Newspaper accounts said that Harris was "a well-known salesman of the Murray Drug Company of Columbia,"[12] "not of a quarrelsome or combative disposition...his friends [had] never heard of him having a quarrel with anyone; neither [had] they ever heard of his carrying a pistol."[13]

The only eyewitness, Captain D. S. DuBois, testified that he was only a few feet from Harris, and that Harris was not armed.[14]

Thurmond was tried for murder and found not guilty. After the verdict, the Yorkville (SC) Enquirer printed this announcement on August 7, 1897:

---

[10] The Edgefield Advertiser, April 14, 1897.
[11] The Watchman and Southron, Sumter, SC, March 31, 1987.
[12] The Fairfield News and Herald, Winnsboro, SC
[13] The Peoples Journal, Pickens, SC, April 1, 1897.
[14] The Manning Times, March 31, 1897.

"Solicitor Thurmond was tried in Edgefield this week for the murder of W. G. Harris. One of the solicitor's bondsmen was foreman of the jury which sat on the case. Acquitted? Why certainly. What else was the trial for?"

In his 1978 interview with James C. Banks, Strom Thurmond had this to say about his father's career after the homicide:

Banks: "Do you think he viewed himself as a success, your father?"

Thurmond: "Well, I don't know whether he did or not. I think, it was unfortunate, one time he had to kill a man. If it hadn't been for that I think he would have been governor or come to the senate or something. After that, I think he probably felt that he was hampered. Although he was appointed--he was solicitor at the time--he shot this man and killed him. And then after that he didn't run, he'd [unknown] but he finished out his term, that was about the middle of his second term. Only later he was appointed here as District Attorney by Woodrow Wilson, so that did not keep him from getting that appointment. Benjamin R. Tillman recommended him for it."[15]

Ben Tillman's nephew, James Tillman, served as one of Thurmond's defense attorneys during his trial for murder. Five years later, James Tillman, who was then the Lt. Governor of South Carolina, shot and killed his unarmed political enemy, the editor of the The State Newspaper, N. G. Gonzales. The trial was moved from Richland County, where Gonzales had a popular following, to Lexington County, where Tillmanites ruled. The prosecutor was none other than Solicitor John William

[15] Interview with Strom Thurmond by James G. Banks, 20 July 1978. A-0334 in the Southern Oral History Program Collection #4007, Southern Historical
Collection, Wilson Library, University of North Carolina at Chapel Hill., page 8.

Thurmond. James Tillman was found not guilty.

2. Young Strom

At the age of ten, Strom Thurmond watched future Governor and Senator Cole Blease give a stump speech during a campaign stop. Young Strom learned a lesson. Blease defeated his opponent because, as Thurmond later recalled, "whoever could make the best speech on the stump was going to get elected."[16] Blease's speeches at the time included the pronouncement that "the Caucasian race must dominate...if an inferior race [gets] in the way it must be gotten out of the way in the most convenient manner. And a little

---

[16] Oral History Interview with Strom Thurmond, July 20, 1978. Interview A-0334. Southern Oral History Program Collection (page #4007) in the Southern Oral History Program Collection, Southern Historical Collection, Wilson Library, University of North Carolina at Chapel Hill.

gunpowder and a few buckshot are often the most effective remedy."[17]

As a youth, Thurmond accompanied his father to his law office, to court, and to visits to the farmlands he managed. After graduating from high school, he went off to Clemson College with several of his friends.[18] Clemson was established due, in large part, to the efforts of his "uncle" Ben Tillman.[19]

In 1923, Strom Thurmond returned home and began teaching in the all-white high schools in McCormick, Ridge Spring, and Edgefield.[20] In a 1924 letter to the editor of the McCormick Messenger, Thurmond wrote "I shall be glad to teach any white adults who have had poor opportunities for an education the

---

[17] The Spartanburg Herald-Journal, July 5, 1911.
[18] Interview A-0334, SOHP.
[19] Biographical Directory of the U. S. Congress.
[20] South Carolina Legislative Manual, 1948.

fundamental principles [of reading and writing], even the alphabet itself."[21]

In 1925, Strom Thurmond and Carrie Butler, the black family maid, had a baby, Essie Mae, who was whisked away to be raised by relatives "up north." Thurmond spent time in Florida that year "selling real estate."[22]

Lynchings were rampant throughout Strom Thurmond's formative years. In neighboring Aiken County, Clarence, Demon, and Bertha Loman were taken from the jail on October 8, 1926 by a large white mob. They were tortured, shot to death, and left lying where they fell. Testimony taken by the grand jury implicated several lawmen, including the Sheriff.[23]

---

[21] Strom Thurmond and the Politics of Southern Change, by Nadine Cohadas, Mercer University Press, 1994.

[22] Edward L. Lach, Jr.. "Thurmond, J. Strom"; http://www.anb.org/articles/07/07-00808.html; *American National Biography Online* July 09-2008; retrieved February 26, 2015.

[23] The Afro-American, January 29, 1927.

Walter White, who headed the national NAACP for 25 years, investigated the case and gave Governor Thomas McLeod the names of dozens of people who participated in the lynching, as well as the names of numerous people willing to testify.[24] The grand jury adjourned without taking action, and no one was ever punished. White South Carolina had a long history of condoning lynching, and the whole nation knew it. The following editorial is reprinted in full from the January 29, 1927 edition of The Afro-American:

South Carolina Accepts Disgrace

South Carolina, where the pendulum of racial relations has swung in history to wider extremes than in any other state in the union, not only disgraces itself but accepts that disgrace with complacency.

---

[24] Ibid.

Study that state if you want to understand some of the deep seated foundations of racial hatred. Pious Yankee financiers of the North who clip cotton mill coupons should understand how their child labor system which has retarded even white education and made much of the colored education only a joke, has contributed to the Aiken horror.

Intelligence, backed up by opportunities for material prosperity is the only cure for South Carolina. There gross ignorance, not of colored men and women but of whites, and blood sucking economic conditions, produce the hatreds out of which lynchings grow.

Poor whites have not yet stopped venting their spleen on colored men in memory of Reconstruction days. The prosperous and right thinking whites are helpless; for where in this country would you find men more outspoken against mob law than the editors of the Columbia daily papers?

Some twenty years ago a Governor of South Carolina[25] *stood on a rail fence platform and begged an unmasked mob to let the law take its course in the case of a colored man they had captured to lynch. They listened until the end of his speech and then immediately proceeded to do the poor wretch to death.*

That a grand jury should even consider seriously convicting white men for mob murder represents some gain in South Carolina. NO WHITE MAN THERE HAS EVER BEEN PUNISHED YET FOR MOB VIOLENCE.

In these times of extreme race hatred and violence, Thurmond was elected to his

---

[25] Refers to Governor Duncan Clinch Heyward's attendance at the lynching of Bob Davis in Greenwood County. Spartanburg Herald-Journal, August 22, 1906.

first political office, Superintendent of Education of Edgefield County. To put things in context, "as a young man, [Strom Thurmond] campaigned for the votes of men who fought in the Civil War."[26]

Thurmond was assisted in his campaign by his companion Sue Logue. He approved of her hiring as a teacher even though another applicant had a college degree. Logue had never attended high school."[27]

As Superintendent, Thurmond focused on health, saying "if you don't have a healthy body, you can't do anything." He focused on medical and dental exams for all school children and courses on health.[28]

---

[26] Congressional Record - Senate, page 7,556, September 24, 2002.
[27] Strom: The Complicated Personal and Political Life of Strom Thurmond, page 59, by Jack Bass and Marilyn Thompson, Public Affairs, Jun 1, 2006.
[28] Oral History Interview with Strom Thurmond, July 20, 1978. Interview A-0334. Southern Oral History Program Collection (page #4007) in the Southern Oral History Program Collection, Southern Historical Collection, Wilson Library, University of North Carolina at Chapel Hill.

His obsession with health lasted a lifetime. He told me many times that one must "take exercise every day." Every time we shared a meal, he explained that "ruffage is very important, you got to eat yo' ruffage."

During this time, Thurmond also studied law in his father's office. He was admitted to the South Carolina bar in 1930, and began working as the Edgefield City and County Attorney.[29]

3.   Early Politics and Near Misses

In 1933, Thurmond was elected to the South Carolina State Senate, where he served until 1938. That year he was elected by his fellow Senators to become a Circuit Judge.

---

[29] South Carolina Legislative Manual, 1948.

Ted Riley was a longtime power player in the South Carolina Democratic Party, and the father of Governor Richard Riley. He had this to say about Strom Thurmond's service as a judge: "As a lawyer with 60 years experience, I think he was, by far, the worst judge that I went up before. I had an arson case before him where a cotton mill had been set on fire and we represented the insurance company. There was a lot of money involved, so it was a pretty important case. Lawyers closed with factual situations and we would hand up the request of charge. There were some pretty intricate problems involved.... Strom read them and it was all Greek to him."[30] Thurmond told the lawyers to work it out and left for lunch.

---

[30] South Carolina Political Collections, Oral History Project, Interview with Ted Riley (1900-1994), by Dr. John J. Duffy and Dr. George D. Terry, October 7, 1986, page 32.

Riley went on to illustrate how Thurmond was in perpetual campaign mode, even as a sitting judge: "To give you an example, I mention Miller Foster from Spartanburg. I was in his office one day and Strom was running for office and I was saying I wasn't going to support him. Miller said, "Ted, we haven't got a chance. You know how long it's been since Strom was a judge. Well, an old mountaineer was in here yesterday, and I was talking to him because he's always been a political ally of mine. He's got family up there with only eight or ten votes in it, but he's the kind that gets around. He said he was going to vote for Judge Thurmond. I asked him what the Judge had ever done for him and he said he would show me. He pulled out a letter addressed to him that called him by his first name. The letter went on to say how much he appreciated his wonderful service to his country by serving as juror at such and such a term of court. Also, that his service would always be remembered and his name would go down in history as a great servant of South Carolina."

"That fellow (Thurmond) sent the same letter to everybody that appeared on the record; defendants, witnesses, lawyers, and jurors. When he would leave a term of court, he got a record from the clerk of court and that letter went to every one of them."[31]

Thurmond presided over two death penalty cases that were cited as examples of black people being denied fair trials in the 2014 re-opening of the South Carolina v. Stinney case.

David Bruck, the well-known and respected authority on the death penalty, wrote an extensively researched work, *The Four Men Strom Thurmond Sent to the Chair*, published in 1981. Bruck's work

---

[31] *Ibid.*, page 33.

was quoted extensively in an *amicus curiae* brief filed in 2014 in the George Stinney case.[32] The fourteen year old Stinney was executed in 1944 after being railroaded by the legal system. In 2014, a South Carolina court ruled that his Constitutional rights had been violated and vacated Stinney's conviction. The following account of how Judge Strom Thurmond handled a similar case is quoted from that amicus curiae brief:

"George Thomas was indicted for the rape of a white woman in 1940 in Georgetown. Immediately after Thomas' arrest, three hundred angry white men armed with rifles and shotguns gathered at the jail. The environment was so charged that the National Guard mounted a machine gun on a second-story balcony to maintain order. Vigilantes roamed black neighborhoods, forcing residents to stay

---

[32] *Amicus curiae* brief, State v. Stinney, February 21, 2014, by Margaret Burnham, Michael Meltsner, and Armand Derfner.

indoors. For his own protection, the defendant was moved on back roads to the state penitentiary in Columbia. Nevertheless, when Thomas' NAACP-retained attorney requested a change of venue, citing the mob violence and a threat to his own life, the trial court [Judge Thurmond] denied the motion. Although Thomas' wife, son, and seven witnesses corroborated his alibi, the all-white jury deliberated for little more than an hour before finding him guilty of rape without recommendation of mercy. Thomas' attorney appealed the conviction, asserting that denial of the change of venue violated the defendant's rights. Although Thomas' counsel's life had been threatened, and Thomas himself had nearly been lynched, faced a packed courtroom, and required a special detachment of thirty-five highway patrolmen for his protection, the conviction (was) affirmed. Thomas was executed in February 1940."

In 1941, Thurmond's career was jeopardized by two separate potential scandals. First, Carrie Butler took their 16 daughter to meet him for the first time. Next, his close friend Sue Logue was charged for paying a hit-man to kill Davis Timmerman as part of an ongoing feud reminiscent of the Hatfields and McCoys.

When Sheriff Ward Allen and Deputy W. L. Clark went to arrest Logue and her brother-in-law George Logue, both lawmen were shot dead. Sheriff Allen, who was unarmed, died on the spot. Deputy Clark returned fire, killing Logue sharecropper Fred Dorn and wounding George Logue.

Deputy Clark and George Logue were taken to separate hospitals; Clark died from his wounds. Sue Logue was still in the house. All of the newspaper accounts of the event agree on everything described so far. Strom Thurmond got involved, and the two versions of what happened next differ significantly.

In Thurmond's version, given in a 1995 interview, "every police officer in Edgefield County was dead or dying. I was the only legally constituted official left to make an arrest."[33] In an earlier interview he said "it was a very Southern crowd, very angry and very mad."[34]

Another report, from 1970, said that: "it was Circuit Judge Thurmond who talked his way past a gun-toting crowd into a cabin fort of more armed men in the climax to the Logue-Timmerman feud. He brought the principle (Sue Logue) out. Thurmond was the only law around."[35]

Eyewitness accounts written by news reporters on the scene painted a much different picture.

---

[33] Spartanburg Herald-Journal, February 5, 1995.
[34] Id., October 2, 1988.
[35] Id., November 4, 1970.

The day after the incident, newspapers reported that there were fifty highway patrolmen on the scene.[36] Lt. J. C. Coleman was the officer in charge. There was "a squad of officers sent here by Governor J. C. Harley headed by Chief Richardson of the state constabulary and Captain L. H. Rourk of the State Prison.[37] *(Author's note: although the State Law Enforcement Division was created in 1935, the term "state constabulary" and "SLED" were used interchangeably well into the 1950's.)*

The Sheriffs of Saluda, Laurens, and Spartanburg Counties were on hand, as well as other lawmen.[38]

According to Lt. Coleman, the crowd "had no apparent mob spirit. They just

---

[36] *Id.*, November 17, 1941.
[37] *Ibid.*
[38] *Ibid.*

wanted to see what was going on," and attributed their presence to "curiosity."[39]

Everyone agrees that Judge Thurmond gave Sue Logue a ride to the State Penitentiary in Columbia. Sue got a change of venue in her trial, just a year after Judge Thurmond denied one for George Thomas in Georgetown.[40]

In remarks in support of a change of venue ruling, Judge G. Duncan Bellinger said "I have listened to the evidence most carefully, and there is no doubt that there is a great deal of feeling on the part of the public in Edgefield regarding this case. I feel that it would be humanly impossible for a panel of Edgefield men to take their place in that jury box and, no matter how hard they try, to erase the feelings that lie there.[41]

---

[39] *Ibid.*
[40] *Id.*, January 6, 1942.
[41] *Ibid.*

"Although it is claimed Strom was pulling wires behind the scenes on her behalf,"[42] Sue Logue was convicted and sentenced to death. Thurmond got to see her one last time.

According to author and Professor Jack Bass, a state employee named Randall Johnson drove Logue from the women's prison to death row about two weeks before her execution. Johnson said that Strom Thurmond, home on leave from the Army, rode in the back seat with her. Johnson later served as Governor Strom Thurmond's driver.

---

[42]Review by Steve Glassman, 2007, on the book Wanton Woman: Sue Logue, Strom Thurmond, and the Bloody Logue-Timmerman Feud, by Anna Flowers, published by iUniverse, Inc. 2007.

4.   In the Army

Judge Thurmond joined the Army when World War II broke out, which gave him needed distance from the near-scandals. Thurmond's service during the war was honorable and heroic. As a circuit judge nearly forty years old, he certainly would not have been expected to serve. Nevertheless, he volunteered at the beginning of the war and stayed until the end.   Thurmond participated in the Normandy invasion on D-Day, assigned to the 82nd Airborne Division. After Germany surrendered he served in the Pacific before returning to South Carolina.[43] Thurmond remained in the Army Reserve, and rose to the rank of Major General.

---

[43] The Strom Thurmond Institute, Biography of Strom Thurmond.

5.   Governor Strom Thurmond

Strom Thurmond returned home from the war and immediately began his campaign for Governor. The homecoming of another soldier to South Carolina brought national shame on the state and set in motion powerful forces that culminated in eventual victories for the national civil rights movement, over the strident and unending objections of Strom Thurmond.

On February 12, 1946, freshly discharged Army Sergeant Isaac Woodard was on his way back home to Fairfield County, having served in the Pacific Theatre during the war. After a disagreement over racial etiquette, the bus driver stopped in Batesburg and told Chief of Police Lynwood Shull that Woodard was causing trouble. Shull beat and jabbed Woodard so bad with a billy club that his eyeballs were ruptured, causing permanent blindness. No one investigated the matter.

After a long stay in the Veteran's Hospital, Woodard went to New York City where he lived the rest of his life.

Despite being ignored in his home state, over the next few months Sgt. Woodard became a national celebrity. Orson Welles blistered Shull and the do-nothing state officials night after night on his national radio broadcast. Woody Guthrie wrote a song about the attack, and had this to say: "I sung 'The Blinding of Isaac Woodard' in the Lewiston (Washington) Stadium one night for more than 36,000 people, and I got the loudest applause I've ever got in my whole life." Joe Louis put on a fundraiser for Woodard, and the US Army gave him a small pension, even though he had technically been discharged just hours before he was blinded.

On September 19, 1946, seven months after the incident, NAACP Executive

Secretary Walter Francis White met with President Harry S. Truman in the Oval Office to discuss the Woodard case. Author Michael Gardner wrote that when Truman "heard this story in the context of the state authorities of South Carolina doing nothing for seven months, he exploded." The following day, Truman wrote a letter to Attorney General Tom C. Clark demanding that the United States Department of Justice open an investigation on the case.[44]

Chief Shull was indicted in federal court for beating Sgt. Woodard.[45] The indictment did not go over well with the South Carolina law enforcement community. The Afro-American reported that "SC Sheriffs and police chiefs are red hot with the Department of Justice, the FBI, and other federal officers because of charges filed against Chief Lynwood L.

[44] theobamacrat.com, July 26, 2013, retrieved January 20, 2015.
[45] The St. Petersburg Times, September 26, 1946.

Shull of Batesburg for blinding Isaac Woodard, Jr. A campaign to bar FBI agents and other federal officers from all future meetings of State and local officers started on Oct. 9, with protest resolutions being filed with Governor [Ransome] Williams of South Carolina, J. Edgar Hoover of the FBI, the attorney general's office, and South Carolina Congressmen.[46]

"By all accounts, the trial was a travesty. The local U.S. Attorney charged with handling the case failed to interview anyone except the bus driver, a decision that [Judge Waties] Waring, a civil rights proponent, believed was a gross dereliction of duty. Waring would later write of his disgust of the way the case was handled at the local level, commenting, "I was shocked by the hypocrisy of my government…in submitting that disgraceful case…."[47]

---

[46] The Afro-American, October 26, 1946.
[47] Wikipedia article, Julius Waites Waring, retrieved March 1, 2015.

The prosecutor "practically apologized" to the jury for trying Shull, saying "I am only doing my job and whatever verdict you gentlemen bring in, the government will be satisfied."[48] During the trial, the defense attorney told the jury that "if you rule against Shull, then let this South Carolina secede again."[49] After Woodard gave his account of the events, Shull firmly denied it, claiming that Woodard had threatened him, and that he had used his nightclub to defend himself. During his testimony Shull admitted that he struck Woodard in the eyes.[50]

On November 5, 1946, the same day Strom Thurmond was elected Governor, the jury found Shull not guilty, putting the state and the treatment of black people, especially black war veterans, in the national news once again.

---

[48] The Afro-American, November 16, 1946.
[49] Ibid.
[50] Ibid.

Exactly one month later, President Truman issued Executive Order 9808 establishing the President's Committee on Civil Rights.[51]

The Wikipedia article about the 1946 election of Strom Thurmond as Governor says "race was not an issue in the campaign." Race may not have been an issue with the all-white electorate that put Thurmond in office, but race most certainly was an issue with black citizens who had attempted to vote in the election, only to be turned away.

South Carolina had repealed all of its election laws two years earlier. When the U. S. Supreme Court ruled that discriminatory election laws in another state were unconstitutional, the state legislature quickly eliminated every single election law in South Carolina so the U. S. Supreme

---

[51] www.trumanlibrary.com

Court couldn't rule likewise. Governor Olin Johnston announced that white supremacy would be maintained.[52] The people in charge of elections said that the Democratic primary, the only election that mattered in South Carolina, was a "private club."[53] "The (South Carolina) Democratic party has as much right to give a ballot to whomever it pleases as does a woman's sewing circle," the party attorney said in a court appearance defending the act of turning away black would-be voters.[54]

The resulting voting rights lawsuit was victorious when, on July 7, 1947, the same Federal Judge who tried to give Isaac Woodard a square deal, Waites Waring, ruled in favor of blacks being allowed to vote.[55] For his stand Judge Waring was exiled from Charlestonian society that his

---

[52] St. Petersburg Times, November 19, 1947.
[53] Ibid.
[54] Ibid.
[55] Wikipedia, Julius Waites Waring article.

family had been a part of since 1683. He retired to New York City and stayed there for the rest of his life.[56]

Three weeks into his term as governor, Thurmond had his own civil rights issue to deal with. On February 17, 1947, a black man named Willie Earle was lynched in Greenville County by a mob of white men who took him from the Pickens County jail and brutally mutilated him, leaving his body lying beside a rural highway.

The FBI and SLED were on the case immediately. Whereas Ben Tillman would have given out medals for such a bold and public lynching, Governor Thurmond condemned the crime and gave orders for SLED to continue the investigation until the case was solved. Within a week, almost all of the suspects had freely admitted to being a part of the lynch mob, and several of them

[56] Ibid.

named the same man as the one who shot Earle in the head with a shotgun.

Despite a solid case that included confessions and eyewitness testimony, all of the men were found not guilty. In an astounding case of jury nullification, the all white jury condoned the lynching. This further widened the gap between the throwback state of South Carolina and the rest of the nation. Despite his proactive handling of the Willie Earle case, the editors of the Afro-American wondered if Strom Thurmond had actually *caused* the murder:

"Mallard, Earle Lynchings Fruit of Racists' Victories, Columbia, S.C. (ANP) -- Parallels in the Nov. 20 lynching of Robert C. Mallard of Toombs County, Ga., and that of Willie Earle, in Greenville County, S.C., of Feb.17, 1947, were noted here this week.

It is being recalled that Earle was lynched less than one month after Governor J. Strom Thurmond, ardent and fiery white supremacist, was inaugurated in late January of 1947. The Mallard lynching has taken place less than one month after the November election of Gov. Herman Talmadge of Georgia.

Thurmond and Talmadge are related by family ties. Both had the support of the Ku Klux Klan in their respective States during the past summer's campaigns."[57]

6.   Running for President

Strom Thurmond embarked on a presidential campaign that opposed federally mandated equal rights for black people. He said it was all about states' rights, and it was. It was about a state's

---

[57] The Afro-American, December 11, 1948.

right to maintain the "customs and traditions" of keeping white people and black people separate and unequal. Two years into his term as governor, Strom Thurmond went head-to-head with President Truman over civil rights and segregation. Thurmond knew the pulse of Southern whites, as demonstrated by this New York Times article from March 6, 1948:

"COLUMBIA, S. C. -- A Valdese, N. C. woman has sent $100 -- in Confederate money -- to Governor Strom Thurmond for the Southern Democratic fight against President Truman's civil rights program. "If our stand on President Truman's civil rights program makes it necessary for us Rebels to secede from the Democratic party and fight the Civil War all over again, I am sure funds will be needed, so I am enclosing my contribution. Please turn it over to the

South Carolina War Department. More power to you!"

One of the major skirmish lines in the 1948 presidential election became the fight over passage of a federal anti-lynching law. Despite the failure of the state legal system in the Woodard and Earle cases, Strom Thurmond vehemently fought against such legislation.

The black community, after lifetimes of no protection against violence in the South, saw things differently. "Dr. Louis T. Wright, Chairman of the National Board of the NAACP, placed the security of a person as 'a basic right' of a free man. All other denials of civil rights are 'secondary,' he asserted. 'If a citizen cannot be protected from physical violence; if he has no refuge in law; if his very life depends upon the whims, prejudices, hatreds and passions of mobs, then he has no security and our democracy as a civilized way of life has no meaning,' Dr. Wright declared. For the sake of the Constitution and the Bill of Rights that we Americans profess to live by, and for the sake of ordinary common justice that is supposed to exist in civilized countries, Congress must enact a Federal anti-lynching law. There have been too many Willie Earles tortured and killed while the Congress of the United States quibbles over technicalities and filibusters this legislation to death."[58]

Southern delegates, Strom Thurmond among them, went to the 1948 Democratic National Convention itching for a fight over President Truman's support of civil rights. Quite a few Southern delegates walked out over the newly adopted civil rights section of the party's platform, which read, in part, "racial and religious minorities must have the right to live, the right to work, the right to vote, the full and equal protection of the

---

[58] New York Times, June 25, 1947.

laws, on a basis of equality with all citizens as guaranteed by the Constitution."[59]

Truman won the Democratic nomination by an overwhelming two-thirds majority.[60]

A small group of Southerners held their own political convention and formed the no-negroes-allowed Dixiecrat party. Harry Truman was busy running against the Republicans, but the Southerners were busy running against Democrat Harry Truman.

Strom Thurmond was nominated as the Dixiecrat presidential candidate, and in his acceptance speech he said: "...there's not enough troops in the Army to force the Southern people to break down segregation and admit the Negro race into our theaters,

---

[59] www.presidency.ucsb.edu.
[60] New York Times, July 15, 1948.

into our swimming pools, into our homes, and into our churches."[61]

The South Carolina Sheriffs' Association issued a statement to the press that said, in effect, the world would come to a certain and violent end if black people were give equal rights:[62]

Sheriff's Association Supports Dixiecrats

Columbia, (AP)—The South Carolina Sheriff's Association put itself on record Wednesday (September 29, 1948) in favor of the States' Rights Democratic movement and in support of the presidential candidacy of Gov. J. Strom Thurmond, the States' Rights Democratic candidate.

In a resolution officers said was adopted unanimously, the sheriffs condemned the civil rights proposals

---

[61] www.columbiasc63.com/civil-rights-timeline, retrieved January 25, 2015.
[62] Spartanburg Herald-Journal, September 30, 1948.

contained in the national Democratic platform and endorsed "the ideals, policies and program of the States' Rights Party."

"ACTIVE SUPPORT" for Thurmond and Gov. Fielding L. Wright of Mississippi, his running mate for vice-president, was pledged.

Sheriffs, the resolution said, "are interested in and responsible for the peace, happiness and general welfare of all the people under their jurisdiction."

"Adoption and enforcement of the so-called civil rights program," the resolution continued, "would result in chaos, hatred, lawlessness and bloodshed...and would abolish all segregation..."

The result would be "usurpation of local law enforcement authority and the breaking down of our peaceful satisfactory racial relations."

Governor Wright, Thurmond's running mate, had this to say to half of the population of his home state of Mississippi: "If any of you have become so deluded as to want to enter our white schools, patronize our hotels and cafes, enjoy social equality with the whites, then true kindness and sympathy requires me to advise you to make your homes in some other state."[63]

In stark contrast, Truman, in July 1948, "over the objection of senior military officers, promulgated Executive Order 9981, banning racial discrimination in the U.S. Armed Forces. This was done as a response to a number of incidents against black veterans, most notably the Woodard case."[64]

Meanwhile, 180 degrees back in South Carolina, Governor Thurmond's staff invited all U. S. governors to visit,

---

[63] Washington Post December 21, 2001.
[64] www.theobamacrat.com, July 26, 2013.

including, inadvertently, the black governor of the Virgin Islands. On October 26, 1948, Thurmond was asked to comment on the accidental invitation and was quoted in the Toledo Blade newspaper as saying "Governor Hastie knows that neither he nor any other Negro will ever be a guest at the Governor's house in Columbia as long as I am Governor..."

Less than a week before the "no negroes allowed" statement, Thurmond told a group of students at University of Georgia, "there's not an ounce of racial hatred in my soul".[65] Apparently, the purposeful, public, and continuous degradation of an entire people to quench his political thirst did not rise to the level of "hatred" in the mind of Strom Thurmond.

Despite his public stance as a devout racist, Governor Thurmond welcomed his

---

[65] Reading (PA) Eagle, October 21, 1948.

bi-racial daughter to the Governor's Mansion.[66]

In October 1948, the *St. Petersburg Times* headlined an article with *"South Carolina Has Seceded Again:"*[67]

"There is about South Carolina the atmosphere of a conquered province. It is in almost complete subjugation to the Dixiecrat movement, for which, of course, it has the self-supplied leader in its own Governor J. Strom Thurmond of whom, however, it has seen little of late. He has been chasing his will o' the wisp, the presidency, all over the South, while his supporters handle things here at home."

"Historic parallels are never exact, nor are historic roles. However, in the Dixiecrats of today there is something of a mock and shabby replica of the "red shirts"

---

[66] CBS Dan Rather interview of Essie Mae Washington-Williams, December 17, 2003.
[67] St. Petersburg Times, October 28, 1948.

of the 1870's who threw off carpet-bagger rule, except for Strom Thurmond, of course, who is no Wade Hampton."

"The tragedy of it all is that this sham revolution should happen in the middle years of the Twentieth Century when the slogans and oratorical flourishes of 85 years ago have such a hollow sound. South Carolina truly has been led back to the past: And the Dixiecrat "red shirts" of today are just as sternly righteous in their attitude, just as over-weening in their arrogance, just as ruthlessly hostile to the free spirit of democracy as were the carpet-bagger regimes of Reconstruction."

"Election methods here smack of those imposed upon a subjugated people. South Carolina has no secret ballot. The ballots are separate, and the voter has to ask for the ballot he wants when he enters the polling place."

"In the situation today in the state, with the Dixiecrats in command, it can be seen how the lack of secrecy can become a species of intimidation. It is feared also that at some polling places the Dixiecrat ballot may be the only one offered the voter. A bill setting up the Australian secret ballot passed the House of Representatives in the last Legislature, but failed of final enactment. Governor Thurmond declined to call a special session to institute it, as was urged to do."[68]

In the November 2, 1948 presidential election, Strom Thurmond received 102,607 votes in South Carolina; Harry Truman received 34,423. It is interesting to note that an estimated 35,000 black South Carolina citizens had been allowed to vote in the 1948 primary election, the first time since the Ben Tillman days.[69] A better

[68] Ibid.
[69] www.uselectionatlas.org, retrieved January 25, 2015.

estimate for the number of black citizens that voted may be 34,423.

Professor Jack Bass played the video of Thurmond's "not enough troops in the Army" speech to him years later. Thurmond responded "we didn't run a racist campaign."[70]

Ninety-two percent of Americans voted against him in his 1948 presidential bid.

7.   Strom Takes Another Flogging

Thurmond enthusiasts portray his winning a few electoral votes as some great victory.   Make no mistake, it may have endeared him to kindred spirits in South Carolina, but the 1948 presidential race was a profound political flogging on the national

---

[70] Southern Oral History Project, Jack Bass Interview, April 15, 2011.

stage. Strom Thurmond began campaigning for the U.S. Senate against Olin Johnston, whom Thurmond branded a "Trumanite" who wanted to "break down all separation of the races."[71] Thurmond was about to be whipped again. This time defeat would come at the hands of black citizens who were able to vote despite Thurmond's continuing attacks on their right to do so.

The South Carolina Democratic Party held the primary on July 11, 1950; Johnston trounced Thurmond. It was estimated that approximately 50,000 blacks voted in the election and they overwhelmingly cast their ballot for Johnston. While the blacks were repulsed by both men's positions on civil rights, they gave their support to Johnston because he had a progressive record and

---

[71] The Whitehouse Looks South, by William Lichtenburg, LSU Press, 2005.

they wanted to penalize Thurmond for his 1948 presidential campaign.[72]

8. Senator for Life

Thurmond had another chance to run for the Senate in 1954. Senator Burnet Maybank died in office, and in a ham-fisted move that alienated virtually every newspaper editor and voter alike, the Democratic Party Executive Committee chose insider Edgar Brown as the party's nominee without calling for a primary election. Sensing the pulse of the voters, Thurmond campaigned as a write-in candidate, reaping the protest votes of all those disaffected by the undemocratic actions of the Democratic Party. Mickey Mouse could have beaten Edgar Brown in

[72] Wikipedia, United States Senate Election in South Carolina in 1950, retrieved February 4, 2015.

that election, and now Strom Thurmond was South Carolina's Senator for Life.

South Carolina dug its heels in on the question of separation of the races. In 1955, the state legislature repealed the compulsory school attendance law to avoid school integration.[73] This way, not even the Supreme Court could force whites to go to school with blacks.

In 1956, Thurmond was re-elected to the Senate and published "The Southern Manifesto," which is exactly what it sounds like: a treatise on the horrors of racial equality.

In 1957 Thurmond filibustered for over 24 hours in protest of the Civil Rights Bill that was up for a vote in the U. S.

---

[73]Afro-American, October 10, 1967.

Senate. When he finally sat down, the bill passed with broad support.[74]

In 1959, Thurmond wrote an editorial piece that complained about Southerners being portrayed as "bigots" and the "persecution of Southern customs and traditions:"[75]

"One of the most important tasks facing the people of the South today is that of piercing the Paper Curtain which has been thrown up by many news media outside Southern borders in an effort to hide or distort the South's position in the segregation-integration controversy. Most Southerners are familiar with the disparaging remarks about us contained in many non-Southern publications and the lack of coverage given our strong points. We are also accustomed to the mammoth headlines given any racial incident in our

---

[74] Wikipedia, the Civil Rights Act of 1957.
[75] The Loris Sentinel, November 11, 1959.

area as contrasted with the lack of display given racial incidents outside the South. Living here in Washington during the Congressional session each year, I can attest to the fact that it is difficult – and in many cases impossible – to find any news articles involving Northern racial flare-ups, which many times outnumber any difficulties we may be having in the South. The Northern editors rationalize the lack of play given these stories on the theory that they do not wish to further stir up racial tensions particularly in the "pilot model" area of Washington, D.C., and in New York City where integration troubles are rapidly making that city the "crime capital" of our nation."

Thurmond goes on to list numerous publications that portrayed, in his opinion, an accurate view of the South, views that would maintain "separate and equal educational facilities for the children of both races." "Outsiders," said Thurmond, were "not familiar with the local customs, traditions, and views" of Southerners.

"The news media in this country are powerful and most influential in molding public sentiment. At the present time most of it is being used against the people of the South. Some of this material is quite open and direct, but some like the recent Loretta Young TV program on prejudice are most clever and subtle, cast the people of the south in the role of appearing to be bigots. I wouldn't say Hollywood has been very kind to us either.

The job of piercing the Paper Curtain and countering this persecution of Southern customs and traditions is a big one, and it merits the attention and consideration of everyone."

After the federal civil rights laws were on the books, Thurmond fought and resisted them and their modifications at every turn. In 1963, Thurmond fought against President Kennedy's public accommodations law that would "make it compulsory to serve and accommodate someone regardless of race, creed, or color."[76]

But the tide was turning. 1963 also marked the year that Harvey Gantt became the first black student enrolled in a public school in South Carolina. To make it even better, Gantt attended Clemson, the college Ben Tillman built, the *alma mater* of Tillman's ideological successor, Strom Thurmond. No doubt Tillman rolled over in his grave every time Gantt walked in the front door of Tillman Hall. Gantt went on to earn an advanced degree from the Massachusetts Institute of Technology. He was twice elected Mayor of Charlotte, N.

---

[76] Ellensburg (WA) Daily Record, July 22, 1963.

C., where he operates a successful architectural firm. The present move to rename Tillman Hall could be abated, perhaps, in favor of placing a statue of Harvey Gantt right out front; it would sort of put things in perspective.

South Carolina was being dragged, kicking and screaming, into the mainstream by Congress and the Supreme Court; but not Strom Thurmond.

Two months after President Lyndon Johnson signed the Civil Rights Act in July 1964, Thurmond switched parties from Democrat to Republican.[77]

In 1965, South Carolina sued the federal government in an attempt to have the Voting Rights Act ruled unconstitutional. It didn't work.

---

[77] Newsweek, July 8, 2014.

In 1967, South Carolina's miscegenation law prohibiting interracial marriage was ruled unconstitutional, along with similar laws in other southern states.[78]

Also that year, Thurmond's old nemesis, Thurgood Marshall, who had spearheaded the NAACP's legal battles in South Carolina and elsewhere, was appointed to the U. S. Supreme Court. Thurmond was the only Republican to vote against Marshall.[79]

In 1968, Strom Thurmond campaigned for Richard Nixon, who had promised Thurmond and other southern governors that he would back a "freedom of choice" school integration plan. "Freedom of choice" was code for "we won't make you go to school with negroes." The South went Republican; "freedom of choice

---

[78] Loving vs. Virginia, US Supreme Court, 1967.
[79] Congressional Record, August 30, 1967.

integration" was shot down by the courts, as expected.

9.   The "Change"

James F. Byrnes (1882-1972) served South Carolina as Governor and U. S. Senator, and served the nation as a Supreme Court Justice and Secretary of State. He once referred to Strom Thurmond as "that energetic idiot," a man who "can do the popular thing, whether its right or not...and he doesn't mind doing it."[80]

Thurmond had always hung his political hat on the notion that the majority of white South Carolina voters were opposed to federally-mandated equal rights for black people. That may have been true, but after the federal government forced

---

[80] Southern Oral History Project, interview with Ted Riley, conducted by Dr. John J. Duffy and Dr. George D. Terry, October 7, 1986.

South Carolina to let everyone vote, despite his skin color, black citizens came to make up 35% of the electorate. Thurmond was slow to acknowledge this new reality.

Although Strom Thurmond had been defeated time and again in his war on the constitutional rights of black citizens, he stuck to his guns and backed fellow traveler Albert Watson for Governor of South Carolina in 1970. This race has been described as the last "openly segregationist campaign in South Carolina,"[81] and the differences in the candidates on the race issue could not have been more dramatic.

In Lamar, S. C., the schools were just then being integrated, *sixteen years* after the U. S Supreme Court ruled in *Brown v. Board of Education* that school segregation was unconstitutional.

---

[81] Greenville Online, March 21, 2004, as quoted in Wikipedia article John Watson, retrieved February 19, 2015.

On February 22, 1970, Albert Watson gave an inflammatory stump speech in Lamar to a group of 2,500 white "freedom of choice" activists, in which he supported their plan to stop integration of the schools. Watson got the crowd riled up, telling them "to ignore those who call you racist, bigot, and hardcore rednecks."[82]

Just nine days after Watson's speech, 200 of those white adults, armed with ax handles and baseball bats, attacked a school bus delivering 39 black children to the Lamar public school. As bricks and rocks smashed the windows, cutting and bruising several of the children, school officials hurried them off to safety as the mob overturned the bus.[83] Thurmond was shouted down at an appearance a few days

[82] Lodi (California) News-Sentinel, March 4, 1970.
[83] *Ibid.*

later when he refused to discuss the Lamar riot.[84]

Watson's opponent, John C. West, by stark contrast, was an idealist who supported racial equality. West soundly defeated Watson, and by extension, Strom Thurmond's white supremacist views. West, in his inaugural address, pledged to "eliminate from our government any vestige of discrimination because of race, creed, sex, religion, or any other barrier to fairness for all our citizens."[85]

Back home in Edgefield, Strom Thurmond High School was in a state of rebellion. Black students resigned from the football team and the band in protest of the school's Confederate mascot, flag, and fight song.[86]

---

[84] Spartanburg Herald-Journal, March 6, 1970.
[85] Afro-American, January 20, 1970.
[86] Sumter Daily Item, October 14, 1970.

Strom Thurmond's staff told him that if he wanted to win reelection, he had better tone down his rhetoric on race.[87]

Thurmond was faced with the certain and utter defeat of his life's work, carrying on "Uncle" Ben Tillman's preservation of the Anglo-Saxon ruling class in South Carolina. Worse, he was faced with the end of his own political power. His burning desire to remain a United States Senator for life was more important to him than rhetoric spoken for public consumption, so he did, in fact, tone it down. Amid a flurry of orchestrated publicity, Thurmond hired his first black staffer. Thereafter, the Senator never missed an opportunity to fly home from Washington to personally announce to groups of black voters that he had obtained federal money for this project or that.

---

[87] Star News, Wilmington, NC, October 4, 2004.

Although it did not gain traction, the story of Thurmond's black family came out during his re-election campaign. Another Edgefield native, W. W. Mims, the editor of The Edgefield Advertiser, used the entire front page with this headline in huge print:

"SEN. THURMOND IS UNPRINCIPLED

---- WITH COLORED OFFSPRING —

WHILE PARADING AS A DEVOUT

SEGREGATIONIST."[88]

Thurmond "exploded in anger," and called the allegation "too scandalous to warrant comment."[89] At the time, Professor Jack Bass was the Columbia bureau chief for The Charlotte Observer. He asked Thurmond about the newspaper headline, and was told "Mr. Bass, do you know that repeating a libel is itself a libel?" He added

---

[88] Ol' Strom, an Unauthorized Biography, by Jack Bass and Marilyn W. Thompson, University of South Carolina Press, 2002.
[89] Spartanburg Herald-Journal, December 12, 2003.

that Mims "had better watch himself" but offered no denial of the allegation...[90]

A generation later, in 1996, I was handed a flyer by my SLED bosses with W. W. Mims' photo on it. The flyer included descriptions of him and his cars, as well as the address of his residence on Courthouse Square in Edgefield. The only instruction was "to keep an eye out for him." Mims was 85 years old at the time. When you get on Strom Thurmond's list, you stay on Strom Thurmond's list.

Thurmond kept right on fighting civil rights legislation, even as he courted the black vote. In a 1974 interview, he said "I'm not a racist, and I've done everything I could to help the people of both races throughout my lifetime."[91]

---

[90] Lincolnplawg Blogspot, quoting Jack Bass' January 3, 2004 article in *The Atlanta Journal-Constitution.*
[91] Times Daily, Florence, Alabama, January 2, 1974.

In 1982, for the first time ever, at the age of 79, after a lifetime of undermining the fundamental rights of black people, over thirty years after the Democratic Party embraced the civil rights movement, Strom Thurmond voted in favor of a civil rights bill before the U. S. Senate.

Strom Thurmond represented South Carolina for another twenty-one years in the U. S. Senate, and he never acknowledged that he had been wrong on the race question. In a 1988 interview, Thurmond blamed the news media for portraying his 1948 presidential campaign as being about race, in spite of the fact that the Dixiecrat Party was formed by Democrats who left the party when Harry Truman called for equal protection under the law for all people.[92]   In 1998, Thurmond was quoted in the Charlotte Observer saying that he still

---

[92] The Legend of Strom's Remorse, by Timothy Noah, Slate Magazine, December 16, 2002.

believed the Dixiecrats were right.[93] The party platform called for a constitutional amendment to outlaw interracial marriage; in his own acceptance speech, Thurmond said "we stand for the segregation of the races, and the racial integrity of each race." Essie Mae Washington-Williams was 23 years old at the time.

Other people say he changed his views on race, but any search for Strom Thurmond himself saying so will come up empty. Strom Thurmond may have been a Teflon legend in South Carolina, but on the national stage he remained toxic on the race issue until the end. At Thurmond's 100th birthday party, Senator Trent Lott of Mississippi said "When Strom Thurmond ran for president, we voted for him. We're proud of it. And if the rest of the country had followed our lead, we wouldn't have had all these problems over the years,

---

[93] http://blogcritics.org/strom-has-apologized-prove-it/

either." Lott was forced to resign his position as the Senate Majority Leader.

10. Constituent Service Machine

Several things gave Strom Thurmond power. He had built up more seniority than any Senator in history. Seniority in Congress causes people to treat you with deference and grant your requests. Add to that the fact that a long line of fellow Republicans occupied the White House during Thurmond's tenure: Nixon, Ford, Reagan, and both Bushes. His tenure gave him access to these Administrations, which added to his power. Thurmond had always been a big supporter of the military. If the Pentagon wanted something, they called Strom Thurmond, and vice-versa. Top off this seniority and access with the best taxpayer-funded perpetual reelection/constituent service machine ever assembled, and you have power.

Strom Thurmond never stopped campaigning. His staff, the largest ever assembled on Capitol Hill, mailed thousands of notes and letters to the folks back home each month.

Everyone in South Carolina knew that if you had a problem with the government, a call to Strom Thurmond's office would get it fixed. Once I met a guy at a festival I attended with the Senator. He told me about his cousin, who was in the Navy, meeting Strom Thurmond when the Senator visited the aircraft carrier he was assigned to. When the Senator asked him about his future plans, he said he would like to be assigned to shore duty on his next tour. A couple of days later, the sailor got word to pack his sea bag immediately and come on deck. A helicopter landed and whisked him away to his new duty station. The Senator's office could cut through virtually any red tape with veterans' benefits, social security, you name it. If you wrote to the Senator about any matter whatsoever you got a response.

The Senator's motto "hep people" worked. It got them what they wanted and needed and it got him re-elected over and over.

11. The Last Hurrah

In the 1990's Strom Thurmond was introduced to a new generation of Americans because of his Chairmanship of the Senate Judiciary Committee. As such, he presided over the controversial confirmation hearings of Supreme Court Justice Clarence Thomas and the impeachment hearings of President Bill Clinton.

Columnist Maureen Dowd wrote about the aging Thurmond in her column: "He is famous for his burnt-umber hair, a forehead tortured by what one reporter tactfully called "semi-successful (hair) transplants" and a mush-mouthed dialect. Dave Barry captured those traits indelibly in a 1991 column lampooning the...hearings: Senator Thurmond: "Soamwhoan ben cudrin' mheah widm tan' bfust drang." Translator: "He says, 'Somebody has colored my hair with what appears to be Tang breakfast drink.' "[94]

Jon Stewart "reported" on Thurmond in the very first airing of The Daily Show: "So far, Strom Thurmond, ears still ringing from the big bang, has emerged as the star of the (President Bill Clinton) impeachment proceedings. Here he is, buzzed from the pitcher of adrenaline juleps needed to keep him alive, swearing in Chief Justice

---

[94] From the column "Old Smoothie," by Maureen Dowd, The New York Times, October 23, 1994.

William Rehnquist. The 96 year old Thurmond did raise some eyebrows when he then turned to Rehnquist and said "I am immortal. I am the Highlander."[95]

Most people thought Strom Thurmond should retire but no one doubted that he would be re-elected in his final election. He refused to debate his opponent, but he made sure that people saw him out and about, making many personal appearances around the state during the campaign.

A fellow SLED Agent drove Senator Thurmond to The Palace Theater at Myrtle Beach in 1996 for a musical variety show featuring Kenny Rogers. The Senator took his seat, and dutifully reviewed the instructional index cards prepared for him by his Washington staff, reading to himself, but aloud, "...stand and wave at crowd." Satisfied and pleased that he knew what to

---

[95] The Daily Show with Jon Stewart, January 11, 1999, in the segment "The Final Blow."

do, he tucked the cards back into his coat pocket and awaited the moment.

The same thing was beginning to happen on Capitol Hill. In a Newsweek article, Weston Kosova wrote that "during meetings, when the discussion veers from his prepared text, he sometimes becomes disoriented. At times he inadvertently reads the stage directions his staff scribbles in the margins, reminding him to pause or look up."[96]

Strom Thurmond's life was in Washington, D.C., and he stayed there until the end of his term, in the final months commuting daily from his room at the Walter Reed Army Hospital. He returned home to Edgefield and died in his sleep a short time later at the age of 100.

---

[96] Strom Thurmond: Home On The Hill--Or Over It?, by Weston Kosova, Newsweek Magazine, May 5, 1996.

When I set out to learn about Strom Thurmond, I found that my history teachers had failed to get through to me the fact that he had spent virtually his entire life fighting against the rights of black people. His run for President, his longest filibuster in history, his Southern Manifesto, and his becoming a Nixon Republican were all undertaken in an effort to protect the "customs and traditions" ingrained in Thurmond in his youth. Whether he was leading or following the electorate could be argued for days. The fact is that he was elected over and over again. Maybe Jimmy Byrnes was right: "He did the popular thing, whether it was right or not, and he didn't mind doing it."

We have made great progress as a people, but many of us have a long way to go, myself included. In 2015, South Carolina Governor Nikki Haley, in a symbolic nod to Ben Tillman and Strom

Thurmond, removed the Poet Laureate from her Inauguration ceremony at the last minute because "there was not enough time" in the program for her to read the poem written specifically for the occasion. Be warned - plan ahead - it takes almost two minutes to read.

One River, One Boat

by Marjory Wentworth, Poet Laureate of South Carolina

"I know there's something better down the road."

– Elizabeth Alexander

Because our history is a knot

we try to unravel, while others

try to tighten it, we tire easily

and fray the cords that bind us.

The cord is a slow moving river,

spiraling across the land

in a succession of S's,

splintering near the sea.

Picture us all, crowded onto a boat

at the last bend in the river:

watch children stepping off the school bus,

parents late for work, grandparents

fishing for favorite memories,

teachers tapping their desks

with red pens, firemen suiting up

to save us, nurses making rounds,

baristas grinding coffee beans,

dockworkers unloading apartment size

containers of computers and toys

from factories across the sea.

Every morning a different veteran

stands at the base of the bridge

holding a cardboard sign

with misspelled words and an empty cup.

In fields at daybreak, rows of migrant

farm workers standing on ladders, break open

iced peach blossoms; their breath rising

and resting above the frozen fields like clouds.

A jonboat drifts down the river.

Inside, a small boy lies on his back;

hand laced behind his head, he watches

stars fade from the sky and dreams.

Consider the prophet John, calling us

from the edge of the wilderness to name

the harm that has been done, to make it

plain, and enter the river and rise.

It is not about asking for forgiveness.

It is not about bowing our heads in shame;

because it all begins and ends here:

while workers unearth trenches

at Gadsden's Wharf, where 100,000

Africans were imprisoned within brick walls

awaiting auction, death, or worse.

Where the dead were thrown into the water,

and the river clogged with corpses

has kept centuries of silence.

It is time to gather at the water's edge,

and toss wreaths into this watery grave.

And it is time to praise the judge

who cleared George Stinney's name,

seventy years after the fact,

we honor him; we pray.

Here, where the Confederate flag still flies

beside the Statehouse, haunted by our past,

conflicted about the future; at the heart

of it, we are at war with ourselves

huddled together on this boat

handed down to us – stuck

at the last bend of a wide river

splintering near the sea.

Addendum

Someone changed SLED's family tree to place Strom Thurmond at the top, and no one noticed.

In 1944, the S. C. Legislative Manual included an entry on SLED for the first time. From 1944 to 1974, the entries stated the same thing: SLED was created by Act 232 of the Legislature in 1935.

In November of 1957, legendary SLED Chief J. P. Strom wrote an article for the *FBI Bulletin* describing SLED's organization and crime-fighting techniques. Strom's article started off by saying that SLED was created in 1935.

SLED's first Chief, J. Henry Jeanes, served from 1935-1941 when he died in office. His death certificate lists his occupation as "Chief, S.C. Law Enforcement Division."

In 1975, the Legislative Manual entry was changed to read that SLED was created in 1947 by Executive Order of then-Governor Strom Thurmond. Subsequent SLED documents state the same. Since then, the new birthday has been printed in newspapers and books, even *The South Carolina Encyclopedia*.

Searching for the Executive Order has been like searching for Bigfoot, the only difference being that people have actually *seen* Bigfoot.

SLED doesn't have it; neither does the S. C. State Archives. Neither does the Strom Thurmond Institute, the official repository of all things Thurmond.

The Institute went even further, stating in a letter to the author that "SLED was not created by a 1947 Executive Order by Governor Strom Thurmond." Archivists there concur that SLED was born in 1935.

It is interesting to note that so far, searches of documents generated during Thurmond's term as Governor and his official biographical information have revealed no instance in which Thurmond himself claimed that he created SLED.

Nevertheless, the new birthday has become so widely accepted that the year *1947* is now cast into SLED badges.

If anyone captures Bigfoot, or the Executive Order, kindly contact the author.